Really Useful English Idioms

D'Arcy Adrian-Vallance

Penguin Quick Guides Series Editors:
Andy Hopkins and Jocelyn Potter

D1390521

Pearson Education Limited
Edinburgh Gate
Harlow
Essex CM20 2JE, England
and Associated Companies throughout the world.

ISBN 0 582 46887 6

First published 2001
Third impression 2003
Text copyright © D'Arcy Adrian-Vallance 2001

The moral right of the author has been asserted.

Produced for the publisher by Bluestone Press, Charlbury, UK.
Designed and typeset by White Horse Graphics, Charlbury, UK.
Illustrations by Anthony Maher (Graham-Cameron Illustration).
Photography by Patrick Ellis.
Printed and bound in China. NPCC/03

Published by Pearson Education Limited in association with
Penguin Books Ltd, both companies being subsidiaries of Pearson plc.

For a complete list of the titles available from Penguin English visit
our website at www.penguinenglish.com, or please write to your local
Pearson Education office or to: Marketing Department, Penguin Longman
Publishing, 80 Strand, London WC2R 0RL.

Contents

Getting
started

What is an idiom?

An idiom is a phrase with a special meaning, like **over the moon** or **pulling someone's leg**. **I'm over the moon** means *I'm very pleased*. **I'm just pulling your leg** means *I'm joking*. When you see or hear an idiom, you may know all the words in it (*over, moon, pull* etc.) but you may not know what the idiom means.

Why are idioms useful?

Idioms are very common in spoken English and informal written English, so it is important – and fun – to learn some of them.

In spoken English, they are used in most situations, from friendly conversations to business meetings.

In written English, they are especially common in newspapers because the writers want to make the headlines and articles interesting and lively.

What will I learn from this book?

You will not learn old-fashioned idioms like **raining cats and dogs**! You will learn idioms that are frequently used in modern everyday English.

This book concentrates on about 130 of the most commonly used idioms.

The idioms are all contained in short, entertaining texts, so that you can easily see the meaning of each idiom and how it is used.

The **Index** at the back lists the idioms in alphabetical order, with further examples, and provides space to write a translation in your own language.

How to use the book

You can just read and enjoy the texts, learning as you read, or help yourself to remember the idioms like this:

- Read a text page and make sure you understand the three (or four) idioms on it.

- Find the idioms in the **Index** at the back of the book and translate them into your language. When you have finished a chapter, think about the review questions at the end of the chapter. You can check your answers in the **Answers** section at the back of the book.

People

1

Types of people

*He was **no rocket scientist** with computers.*

Does it matter if someone says you're **no rocket scientist**? Yes, it does! This phrase means *not very intelligent*.

What if a newspaper describes a politician as a **dark horse**? This means *nobody knows much about him*.

And a **party pooper**? This means a *person who spoils enjoyable activities by refusing to join in*. This idiom is also useful in apologies: 'I'm sorry to be a party pooper, but I have to go home now.'

no rocket scientist
not very intelligent person

dark horse
secretive person

party pooper
person who spoils fun

Brains and beauty

*Her car **turned** almost as many **heads** as she did.*

A Hollywood actress once met the British philosopher, Bertrand Russell. Whereas he was quite ugly, she **turned heads** wherever she went. She was rather **full of herself** and said to Russell, 'They say I'm the most beautiful woman in the world, and I hear you're the smartest man. Imagine if we had a child with your brains and my beauty.'

Russell, who was never **lost for words**, replied, 'Imagine if it had my beauty and your brains.'

turn heads
attract a lot of attention

full of yourself
too pleased with yourself

lost for words
not knowing what to say

Larger than life

*James Bond, the **larger-than-life** secret agent, was first played by Sean Connery.*

Say 'Sean Connery' to **the man in the street** and he'll probably say 'James Bond'. The famous British secret agent, 007, has been played by six actors in the last forty years, but Connery was the original and probably the best. He was **larger than life** both on the screen and **in the flesh**. Even in his 60s, he was chosen by the readers of an international women's magazine as *The World's Most Attractive Man*.

the man in the street
an average person

larger than life
more exciting than normal

in the flesh
as a real person

Twins

Some twins are identical, but my brother and I are definitely not. He's a **couch potato** who watches television all weekend and thinks exercise is a **dirty word**, whereas I'm always **on the go**, playing sport, socialising, working and so on. He says I'm a **pain in the neck** because I never stop doing things and making a noise while he's trying to watch the TV or sleep.

couch potato
a lazy person

dirty word
something unpleasant

on the go
active

pain in the neck
a nuisance

Review 1

A Match the idioms with their meanings.

1 larger than life   a) obscure person
2 dark horse   b) exciting
3 on the go   c) active, busy

B Complete the idioms.

1 She was so surprised that she was lost .....
2 He's too full .... to be interested in us.
3 My little brother is a pain .... sometimes.
4 The man .... cares more about money than politics.

C Think about real people ...

1 Is there a couch potato in your family?
2 Do you know someone who turns heads?
3 Have you ever seen a film star in the flesh?
4 Have you ever been a party pooper?

Emotions

All kinds

*I'm sorry, Charles, but classical music just **leaves me cold**.*

Anger, happiness, love, hate, fear, boredom – whatever you feel, there's an idiom to put it into words. And if something doesn't excite you at all, you can say, it **leaves me cold**.

You can express moderate feelings such as I'm **on edge** (which is how you might feel before making a speech or having a tooth out), or strong feelings, such as, I was bor**ed to death**. I was worri**ed to death**. I was scar**ed to death**.

leaves me cold
has no effect on me

on edge
anxious

(-ed) to death
extremely (-ed)

Laughter

*Everyone was **in stitches**.*

Somebody told a very funny joke at the office yesterday, and we were all **in stitches** for five minutes afterwards. Then the boss came in. He was in a bad mood and started to talk about a work problem. I couldn't forget the joke and I couldn't **keep a straight face**. The boss asked me what I was smiling at. When I told him, he just looked at me and said nothing. I thought he was going to throw me out. But then he **burst out laughing**!

in stitches
laughing a lot

keep a straight face
not smile or laugh

burst out laughing
suddenly laugh loudly

Happiness

He was **over the** **moon**.

It's a beautiful day, and I feel **on top of the world**!

He's just had some good news. He's got the job that he wanted, and he's **over the moon** about it.

Getting my first job as an actor was so exciting. I was **on cloud nine** for weeks afterwards.

on top of the world
happy

over the moon
very pleased about something

on cloud nine
very happy because of something

Road rage

What's got into him?

ROAD RAGE

As roads become busier, road rage is becoming more common. Ben Smith, 43, from London, was trying to park his car yesterday when another driver got in first. Smith **saw red**, jumped out, shouted at the other driver and started kicking the man's car, doing £800 worth of damage. Smith told police later, 'I don't know **what got into me**. I've never done anything like that before. I just **lost it**.'

see red
suddenly feel extreme anger

what got into him
why he became so extreme

lost it
lost control

Broken heart

*She **broke his heart** when she said goodbye.*

Almost as soon as he met her, he fell **head over heels** for her. They had six wonderful months together, and then she left. It **broke his heart**, and a year later he's only beginning to **pick up the pieces**.

head over heels

suddenly and deeply in love

break someone's heart

make someone very sad

pick up the pieces

rebuild something that was damaged

Review 2

A Match the idioms with their meanings.

1 on edge   a) laughing a lot
2 in stitches   b) feel very angry
3 lose it   c) anxious
4 see red   d) be out of control

B Complete the idioms.

1 I feel on top .... when the sun shines.
2 She burst .... when she saw me.
3 I'm on cloud .... whenever we're together.
4 He suddenly hit me. I don't know what
    .... him.

C Can you remember a time when you …

1 were scared to death?
2 saw a film that left you cold?
3 couldn't keep a straight face?
4 were over the moon about something?

Social
relations

3

Party!

*They really **pushed the boat out** for their daughter's wedding.*

I went to a big party last night. The hosts were celebrating something so they'd decided to **push the boat out**: there was a really good band, fantastic food and lots of drink. I chatted to a few people for the first hour – just the usual **small talk**. Then I met this great guy. We got talking and we really **hit it off**. I'm seeing him tomorrow!

push the boat out
spend more than usual

small talk
polite conversation about unimportant things

hit it off
like each other

A good friend

*Even best friends don't **see eye to eye** on everything.*

A good friend

- is someone who will always **be there for** you when you need them.

- is someone who **sees eye to eye** with you on most things.

- is not perfect and not the same as you, but is good at **give and take**.

be there for
be ready to help

see eye to eye
agree

give and take
compromise and cooperation

What to say

*The dinner's **on me**.*

How can you say 'no' to an invitation for now but keep the invitation open for another time?

• Can I **take a rain check**?

What can you say if someone invites you to an event that is dependent on something else, such as good weather.

• (Let's keep our) **Fingers crossed**.

And if someone offers to pay for drinks or a meal, but *you* want to pay?

• This is **on me**.

take a rain check
keep an invitation open

fingers crossed
let's hope for the best

on me
I'll pay

People at work

*The new secretary is **a breath of fresh air**.*

Old Mr Brown has been with the company for years. He's pretty useless, but he survives because the manager **has a soft spot for** him.

There are two bossy middle-aged women who are always **at each other's throats** about one thing or another.

There's a nice girl who started last week and is a **breath of fresh air**.

have a soft spot for
like, care about

at each other's throats
arguing

breath of fresh air
pleasantly different

Review 3

A Match the idioms with their meanings.

1 see eye to eye   a) like each other
2 it's on me   b) let's hope
3 hit it off   c) I'll pay
4 fingers crossed   d) agree

B Complete the idioms.

1 The nice new secretary was a breath .....
2 No. You paid last time. This is on .....
3 I think he has a .... for you.
4 I can't come out tonight, but can I take ....?
5 Give .... is important in a good relationship.

C Think about your social life ...

1 Are you good at small talk?
2 Do you try to be there for your friends?
3 When did you last push the boat out?

Dating
and
romance

4

She likes me!

TOM: I think she likes me.

SAM: **In your dreams!**

TOM: No, really, I'm sure she does.

SAM: **No way!** She never even looks at you.

TOM: Exactly! That means one of two things: either she's embarrassed because she fancies me, or she's **playing hard to get**.

SAM: Tom, there is a third possibility …

In your dreams.
it's a very unrealistic hope

no way
definitely not

play hard to get
pretend to be uninterested

Gossip

No, **he's** history. She's got a new boyfriend.

ETHEL: Have you heard about Jane's boyfriend?

MAVIS: The one she's been **going steady** with for about six months?

ETHEL: No. **He's history**. She's got a new one.

MAVIS: That's fast!

ETHEL: Yes. And he's younger than her! Oh! Hello, Jane.

JANE: Haven't you got anything better to do than gossip about other people? **Get a life!**

going steady
in a regular relationship

he/she's history
past, not important now

get a life
(not polite) do something interesting

Drop-dead gorgeous

*Everyone thinks he's **drop-dead gorgeous**.*

Your letters

Dear Romance Magazine

My boyfriend is **drop-dead gorgeous**, kind and sensitive, and we have a great relationship. He's also very tall. (I **have a thing about** tall men, so that's important to me too!) The problem is that I want to get married and have children, but he doesn't. I love him, but I know he's never going to **pop the question**. What should I do?

Julie (London)

drop-dead gorgeous
very attractive

have a thing about
like very much

pop the question
ask 'Will you marry me?'

Love at first sight

*It was **love at first sight**.*

There is a romantic story about the nineteenth-century revolutionary, Garibaldi. He was on his ship entering a port when he saw a beautiful woman standing on the shore. 'That is the woman I am going to marry,' he said. It was **love at first sight**. The woman, when she met him, was **swept off her feet** by his good looks and personality. They were married within days and **only had eyes for** each other for the rest of their lives.

love at first sight
falling in love immediately

sweep someone off their feet
make them fall in love quickly

only have eyes for
only be interested in

Dating dilemma

Do you fancy **going Dutch**?

On a first date, who should pay for meals, drinks, tickets etc.? In the old days, the man would **pick up the tab**, but nowadays nobody is quite sure. Will the woman think he's a dinosaur if he pays? Or will she think he's mean if he doesn't? Will the man be grateful if the woman suggests they **go Dutch** or will he be insulted? There's no right answer. You just have to **play it by ear**. Be sensitive to your partner's feelings and you'll probably get it right.

pick up the tab
pay the total

go Dutch
share costs on a date

play it by ear
not follow a plan

Review 4

A Match the idioms with their meanings.

1 no way
2 go steady
3 he's history
4 go Dutch

a) share costs
b) definitely not
c) in a regular relationship
d) in the past

B Complete the idioms.

1 As soon as they met it was love .....
2 He took out a ring and popped .....
3 Some people plan, others play it .....
4 He's in love and only has .... for her.

C Do you know someone who ...

1 is drop-dead gorgeous?
2 plays hard to get?
3 never picks up the tab?

D Look at the pictures on this and the next page. Complete the idioms.

1 Man: 'Come and have a drink with me.'
Woman: 'In ....!'

2 All Andy's girlfriends have had ponytails. I
guess he has a .... ponytails.

Life
situations

5

Lottie's diary

You'll find **Mr Right** one day, dear.

I finished reading 'Bridget Jones's Diary' by Helen Fielding today. It's a very popular book, and I loved it because Bridget and I are **in the same boat**: we're both looking for **Mr Right** (without success) and trying to become famous in our careers (without success), and we're both sure that we'll get there as soon as we can lose weight, get fit and generally **get our act together**.

in the same boat
in the same situation

Mr Right
the ideal man

get your act together
prepare yourself for action

In hot water

hot water
trouble

in your shoes
in your situation

off the hook
out of trouble

MIKE: Tom's in **hot water**.

JAKE: Why? What's he done?

MIKE: He borrowed a company car without permission and smashed it up.

JAKE: Is he OK?

MIKE: Yes, he's fine, but I wouldn't like to be **in his shoes** when the boss finds out.

JAKE: Oh, he'll make up a good story and get **off the hook**. He always does.

Country life

*She was pleased to escape from the **rat race**.*

After five years of **life in the fast lane**, Janie decided to give up her well-paid city job and start a new life in a small country village. But although she was pleased to escape from the **rat race**, she felt like a **fish out of water** in the country. Now she's back in the city, wiser for her experience.

life in the fast lane
fast, high-pressure lifestyle

rat race
competitive working life

fish out of water
uncomfortable in a strange situation

Team on a roll

keep your head above water
survive

on a roll
enjoying continual success

put your feet up
relax

TEAM ON A ROLL

After a difficult start to the competition, when England did well to **keep their heads above water** in the match against the very strong Brazilian team (result: 1–1), the England team have been **on a roll**, winning every match including last night's spectacular game which ended in a 3–0 win. However, they can't afford to **put their feet up** because the next match will be the hardest yet.

*England made the mistake of **putting their feet up** too early.*

Review 5

A Match the idioms with their meanings.

1 Mr Right   a) relax
2 hot water   b) trouble
3 put your feet up   c) the ideal man
4 off the hook   d) out of trouble

B Complete the idioms.

1 We're in the ...., so let's help each other.
2 You need to get your .... and find a job.
3 He left the rat .... to work in the third world.
4 How would you feel if you were in my ....?

C Which of these is negative?

1 putting your feet up
2 feeling like a fish out of water
3 being on a roll

Conversation

6

A film scene

Hugh Grant realises he has **put his foot in it**.

In the film *Four Weddings and a Funeral*, Hugh Grant meets an old friend, and asks him, 'How are you, and how's your girlfriend?'

The man replies, 'She's not my girlfriend any more.'

'That's good,' says Grant, 'You probably didn't know, but she was **two-timing** you with someone else.'

The man looks deeply shocked and says, 'She's my wife now.'

Hugh Grant realises he has **put his foot in it**, and he **kicks himself** for being so stupid.

two-timing
deceiving, being unfaithful

put your foot in it
unintentionally upset someone

kick yourself
feel angry with yourself

Can you keep a secret?

*Don't **let the cat out of the bag**.*

A friend has just told you a secret. Then someone asks, 'What were you two talking about?' Do you …
(a) smile and just say mysteriously, '**That would be telling**'?
or (b) **spill the beans**?

Your friends are planning a surprise party for someone. Do you …
(a) keep your mouth shut until the party?
or (b) **let the cat out of the bag** the day before?

That would be telling.
it's a secret

spill the beans
reveal a secret

let the cat out of the bag
give secret information too early

Opinions

Is B agreeing or disagreeing?

A: He talks too much.

B: **You're telling me**! I sat next to him on the bus yesterday!

A: It's hot today, isn't it?

B: **You can say that again**.

A: He's an intelligent boy; the real problem is that he's lazy.

B: I think you've **hit the nail on the head**.

You're telling me.
I know that

You can say that again.
I agree strongly

hit the nail on the head
describe something accurately

Believe me!

*I'm not **pulling your leg!***

SAM: Hello?

TOM: Sam! Help me!

SAM: What's the matter, Tom?

TOM: I'm hanging from this rock by one hand. I can't hold on much longer. Call the rescue service quickly!

SAM: Very funny, Tom. Why are you always **pulling my leg**?

TOM: Sam! I'm not **having you on**. It's true! Honestly!

SAM: **Pull the other one**, Tom!

pull someone's leg
teasing me

have someone on
say something untrue (for fun)

pull the other one
I don't believe you

Hot ears

It was
uncomfortable,
to say the least.

Have you heard this joke?

A: My ears got burnt!

B: How?

A: I was ironing when the phone rang. Instead of picking up the phone I picked up the iron.

B: That must've hurt!

A: **To say the least**.

B: Let's **get this straight**: you said you burnt both ears. Right?

A: Yes.

B: How **on Earth** did you burn the other ear?

A: The person called again.

to say the least
very much

get it straight
be clear about it

on Earth
I can't imagine

Review 6

A Match the idioms with their meanings.

1 two-time   a) reveal a secret
2 spill the beans   b) be unfaithful
3 You're telling me. c) teasing me
4 pulling my leg   d) I know that

B Complete the idioms.

1 Look! A spider behind you! – Pull .....
2 What's the secret? – That would .....
3 This is difficult. – You can .....
4 It tastes like a Bordeaux. – You've hit .....

C Which feels the worst?

1 kicking yourself for forgetting something
2 putting your foot in it
3 realising that someone is having you on
4 letting the cat out of the bag by mistake

Thinking
and
learning

7

Predictions

*I thought you said he was a **safe bet**.*

Who is most optimistic? Who is most pessimistic?

CHRIS: I think we might get a good pay rise this year.

SAM: **That'll be the day!**

TOM: I think it's **on the cards**.

HELEN: I think it's a **safe bet**. The company's made a big profit this year.

KATE: You're right, but it's still **touch and go** whether they'll share it with us.

---

that'll be the day
it would be very surprising

on the cards
likely

safe bet
almost certain

touch and go
unsure

Memory

He suddenly realised that the speaker's name had **slipped his mind**.

A woman was having dinner with a friend and her husband, when she noticed that her friend always called her husband loving names like *Honey, Darling, Sweetheart* etc. While her husband was out of the room, the woman said, 'It's 70 years since you two **tied the knot** but you still call him those pet names. That's wonderful. It must **take some doing** to keep romance alive for so long.' Her friend answered, 'The truth is that his name **slipped my mind** about ten years ago.'

tie the knot
get married

take some doing
not be easy

slip your mind
forget

Pronunciation

Your Cocobanana Cocktail Sir !

*Boris thought he was **getting the hang of** the language until he tried ordering a cup of coffee.*

A **golden rule** of pronunciation is: use word stress correctly.

You probably know that one part of a word is 'stressed' (= stronger than the other parts), for example: PHOtograph, phoTOgrapher, photoGRAPHic.

Listen for the stress in words. Then you'll **get the hang of** word stress and be able to use it more. If you can do this, your pronunciation will improve **just like that**.

golden rule
important rule

get the hang of
learn how to do/use something

just like that
quickly and easily

Listening

I can't **make head nor tail of** it.

Learners of English sometimes say, 'I don't listen to English on the radio because it's too fast and I can't **make head nor tail of** it.

But think about that. When you were a few months old, learning your own language **from scratch**, did you understand it all? No! But you listened and learned. Then you learned to speak and read and write. But listening came first. So even if you don't feel confident, **have a go** at it.

(can't) make head nor tail of
(can't) understand

from scratch
from the beginning

have a go
have a try

Fear of flying

*The steward's attempt to calm the passengers would have **carried more weight** if he had removed his parachute.*

Statistics prove that flying is a very safe method of transport, but this **cut no ice** with Jean Fellows, 60, and nobody could persuade her to try to overcome her lifelong fear. That was until her seven-year-old granddaughter told her to be brave and try. It is unusual for the words of a child to **carry** more **weight** than those of adults, but Jean **took** them **to heart** and finally bought an air ticket. 'It wasn't as bad as I thought,' she said after the flight.

cut no ice
have no influence

carry weight
have influence

take to heart
consider seriously

Review 7

A Match the idioms with their meanings.

1 touch and go   a) unsure
2 on the cards   b) get married
3 tie the knot   c) try
4 have a go   d) likely

B Complete the idioms.

1 We'll have to start again from .....
2 Some people can memorise phrases just .....
3 A golden .... of learning is to practise regularly.
4 It's a safe .... that I'll forget some of these idioms.
5 I couldn't swim at the beginning of the course but now I'm getting .....

C Complete the idioms on this and the next page.

1 Mother: 'Is your room clean and tidy?'
  Father: 'Ha ha! That'll be ....!'

2 I don't understand adults. I explained that I couldn't do the homework because of an important party last night, but it cut .... with him at all.

Action

8

Sleepy burglar

*He was **caught red handed** when the owners came home.*

This is a true story about a French burglar. After getting into an empty house easily through an open window, he probably thought his job was a **piece of cake**. He decided to **take his time** and went into the kitchen, where he found some champagne. After drinking the whole bottle, he went to look for jewellery in the bedroom but fell asleep on the bed. He did not wake up until the owners returned, **catching him red handed**.

piece of cake
very easy

take your time
don't hurry

catch someone red handed
catch someone doing something bad

Action hero

*You have to look good **in the thick** of the action.*

Action movie heroes may seem strong and independent, but they have to follow rules:

1 Never do things **by the book**. Forget about correct procedures.

2 Always wait till the last possible moment before **turning the tables** on the bad guys.

3 When you're **in the thick of** the action, your hair and make-up still have to look good.

by the book
following the rules

turn the tables
reverse the situation

in the thick of
in the most active part

Sports idioms

An **own goal**.

From British football:

The government has **scored an own goal** by reducing tax at a time when it needs extra money.

From American baseball:

It would be nice to exchange news. Let's **touch base** next week.

From boxing:

The gloves are off in this political campaign, with both candidates using personal attacks and dirty tricks.

score an own goal
harm yourself

touch base
get in contact

the gloves are off
the fight is very aggressive

Losing weight

Step on it!

Today was going to be the day that I started to lose weight. Well, I went for a run in the park with Victoria. I thought that would **do the trick**, but it nearly killed me. She kept looking back and telling me to **step on it**. It's no good. I've left it too late. Once you're over 30, you've **missed the boat**. I'm just going to get fat and enjoy it. Now, where are those chocolates that I threw away?

do the trick
solve the problem

step on it
go faster

miss the boat
be too late

Job on the line

*Your job's **on the line** if you can't get **on top of** this problem.*

Bill had a problem waking up in the mornings. One day his boss said angrily, 'You're late for work every day. You probably think I'm a **soft touch**, but I'm not, and your job's **on the line**.'

So Bill went to his doctor, who gave him a pill, which Bill took before he went to bed.

He slept well and woke up early. Arriving at work, he said, 'Boss, I'm **on top of** the problem!'

'That's fine,' said the boss, 'but where were you yesterday?'

soft touch
easy to get things from

on the line
at risk

on top of
in control of

Review 8

A Match the idioms with their meanings.

1 piece of cake   a) go faster
2 take your time   b) easy
3 step on it   c) don't hurry
4 miss the boat   d) be too late

B Complete the idioms.

1 The police caught the thief red .....
2 The campaign has started, and the gloves .....
3 We made a mistake and scored .....
4 The doctor said, 'These pills will do .....'

C Can you think of a film in which ...

1 the police don't do things by the book?
2 the hero turns the tables on the baddies?
3 the hero is always in the thick of the action but is never hurt?

Work
and
business

9

Business success

Joe **made a killing** when the spider-men visited Earth.

DOT.COM SUCCESS

Two young entrepreneurs, who started a new Internet business two years ago, have today sold the business for £3 million. Jenny Curtis, co-founder of Slimmm.com, says, 'Everyone thinks we've **made a killing**, but it was hard work. For the first 18 months we couldn't **make ends meet** – I couldn't even buy a new pair of socks! When the business finally **got off the ground**, we worked 18 hours a day for six months.'

make a killing
make a big profit quickly

make ends meet
pay for necessities

get off the ground
start to be successful

Job interviews

*Most interviewers **make up their minds** in the first 30 seconds.*

Interviewers always ask difficult questions that nobody could possibly answer **off the cuff**. So it's important to be prepared for them. But you can't prepare for everything, so sometimes you just have to **think on your feet**. Don't worry if you make a few mistakes. Just remember what the psychologists tell us: most interviewers **make up their minds** in the first 30 seconds anyway.

off the cuff
without preparation

think on your feet
think as you go along

make up your mind
make a definite decision

B.I.G. in the red

I know we're **on a shoestring**, but this is crazy!

B.I.G. IN THE RED

Profits are down this year for the multinational B.I.G. Co, and figures show the company is **in the red**. B.I.G.'s chief executive says, 'A slowdown in the world economy means that a lot of companies are **feeling the pinch**. Many are cutting their expenses and trying to operate **on a shoestring**, but we're big enough to keep going normally, and we'll be back **in the black** next year.'

in the red/black
in debt/credit

feel the pinch
begin to feel poor

on a shoestring
with little money to spend

A new job

*On her first day, the new gardener was still **finding her feet**.*

When you start a new job, it takes some time before you feel confident about what to do and how to do it. Ideally, an employer recognises this and allows you to **find your feet** before taking on anything too difficult. But life is not always ideal, so you may be thrown **in at the deep end** and have to **sink or swim**.

find your feet
get used to a new situation

in at the deep end
directly into a difficult job

sink or swim
survive without help

Big fish

MANAGER

*She's trying to **get** some **big fish** on board.*

When Herman came to Britain to work, he spoke good English but did not know many idioms. One day at work someone said, 'Don't disturb the manager. She's meeting some **big fish** from New York.'

'Big fish?' Herman asked.

'Yes, she's got a new project and she wants to get them **on board**.'

As Herman reached for his dictionary of English idioms, an extraordinary picture formed in his **mind's eye**.

big fish
important people

on board
actively involved

mind's eye
imagination

Review 9

A Match the idioms with their meanings.

1 off the cuff
2 in the red
3 big fish
4 mind's eye

a) imagination
b) without preparation
c) owing money
d) important person

B Complete the idioms.

1 I must choose, but I just can't make up .....
2 He started the business at home on a .....
3 It takes a few days to find .... in a new job.
4 My salary is very low, and I can't make .....

C Are these things good or bad for a business?

1 being in the black
2 feeling the pinch
3 making a killing

D Look at the pictures on this and the next page. Complete the idioms.

1 You've had the training. Now you have to ..... .

2 The new business got .... quickly.

That's
bad!

10

Bad things

Mind your own business!

We often use idioms when we react to bad things. For example, 'That's **below the belt**' means someone has said something unfair and cruel in an argument. Idioms can also show that a speaker does not like something: 'Bob's **sitting on the fence**' means Bob is refusing to give an opinion, which is not necessarily bad, but the speaker thinks it is. Some idioms are direct and impolite, such as '**Mind your own business**!' which means 'This is private. Keep your nose out of it.'

below the belt
unfair and cruel

sit on the fence
be neutral

mind your own business
this is private

Bad or not?

*The builders **cut corners**? What do you mean? It looks great to me.*

Your employer says you must finish some work by tomorrow. Is it OK to **cut corners**, or would you work **around the clock** to do the work properly?

What would you do if somebody offered to **pull strings** to help you get into a good university or to get a good job?

What if a friend of yours commits a crime? Would you tell the police or **turn a blind eye**?

cut corners
do incomplete work

around the clock
for 24 hours a day

pull strings
use influential friends

turn a blind eye
ignore it

Poison

*The debate began to **get out of hand.***

Winston Churchill was famous for, amongst other things, his quick wit. On one occasion in parliament, the opposition party was **up in arms** because Churchill's government had given the **thumbs down** to a proposed new law. The debate began to **get out of hand** and a woman shouted, 'If I were your wife, I'd give you poison.' Churchill instantly replied, 'If you were my wife, I would drink it.'

up in arms
protesting strongly

thumbs down
negative response

get out of hand
get out of control

Embarrassing!

*All his usual jokes **fell flat**.*

I was working as a tour guide and I was having a difficult time with a group of elderly ladies. None of my attempts to **break the ice** were working, and all my usual jokes were **falling flat**. I didn't know what to do to cheer them up.

A bit later I was getting out of the bus and I tripped and fell and tore my trousers. The ladies almost **split their sides** … and after that, everything was fine!

break the ice
create a relaxed atmosphere

fall flat
fail

split their sides
laughed uncontrollably

Kiss and tell

*He knew **his** days were numbered.*

KISS AND TELL

The latest disaster for the government is the **kiss-and-tell** story in yesterday's *Sunday World* newspaper, in which a well-known actress told of her two-year affair with the Minister for the Family. As the man who **calls the shots** in the government's policy on family values, the Minister's **days are numbered**, and the government's credibility has been severely damaged.

kiss-and-tell
telling the details of a love affair

call the shots
to be the decision maker

days are numbered
survival is unlikely

Review 10

A Match the idioms with their meanings.

1 below the belt   a) ignore it
2 up in arms   b) unfair, cruel
3 turn a blind eye   c) protesting
4 fall flat   d) fail

B Complete the idioms.

1 Powerful people can get things by pulling .....
2 The plan got the thumbs .... from the director.
3 The country has a king, but he doesn't call .....
4 A friendly greeting helps to break .....

C Do you ...

1 express your opinions or sit on the fence?
2 gossip or mind your own business?
3 cut corners sometimes?
4 ever work around the clock?

D Look at the pictures on this and the next page. Complete the idioms.

1 They laughed so much, they almost .....

2 By 6 pm, the party was getting .....

Index

Your language

around the clock
Airports are open around the clock.

_____

at each other's throats
What's that noise? Are they at each other's throats again?

_____

below the belt
I know you were angry, but that comment was below the belt.

_____

be there for
My parents are great. They've always been there for me.

_____

big fish
He's a big fish now that his company's successful.

_____

break someone's heart
Losing him broke her heart.

_____

break the ice
He told a joke to break the ice at the beginning of his speech.

_____

Your language

breath of fresh air
*In an office full of boring people,
she was like a breath of fresh air.*
_____

burst out laughing
*He looked angry, but suddenly
burst out laughing.*
_____

by the book
*The police can't do whatever they
want; they have to go by the book.*
_____

call the shots
*Britain lost her empire long ago
and no longer calls the shots.*
_____

carry weight
*He is an expert, so his opinions
carry a lot of weight.*
_____

catch someone red handed
*The police caught him red handed
inside the bank at midnight.*
_____

couch potato
*Couch potatoes, who don't use
their minds or bodies, risk ill health.*
_____

Your language

cut corners
We'll have to cut corners if we're going to finish the job in time.

_____

cut no ice
I thought I had a good excuse, but it cut no ice with my boss.

_____

dark horse
The new director is a dark horse. I wonder what he's like.

عا مس ن رکتوم

days are numbered
When the lion came towards him, he thought his days were numbered.

_____

dirty word
Love became a dirty word during the Chinese cultural revolution.

_____

do the trick
This medicine should do the trick.

_____

drop-dead gorgeous
He's not just good-looking, he's drop-dead gorgeous.

_____

Your language

get a life
*Why don't you do something
exciting? Get a life!*
_____

get it straight
*Let's get this straight. I'm in charge
here. You follow me.*
_____

get off the ground
*If we can get this idea off the
ground, we'll be rich.*
_____

get out of hand
*The demonstration got out of hand
and twenty people were injured.*
_____

get the hang of
*Keep practising and you'll soon get
the hang of it.*
_____

get your act together
*I must get my act together and
find a good job.*
_____

give and take
*If you want an agreement, you
have to accept some give and take.*
_____

Your language

have someone on
You're not really a police officer, are you? You're having me on.

_____

head over heels
She met him on holiday and fell head over heels for him.

_____

he's/she's history
She used to go out with him, but he's history now.

_____

hit it off
Mothers don't always hit it off with their son's girlfriends.

_____

hit the nail on the head
'This wine tastes like a Bordeaux.' – 'You've hit the nail on the head.'

_____

hot water
His extreme opinions are always getting him into hot water.

_____

in at the deep end
There was a crisis on my first day, so I was thrown in at the deep end.

_____

Your language

in stitches
*The speaker was so funny that the
audience were in stitches.*

_____

in the flesh
*I've seen him on TV, but not in the
flesh.*

_____

in the red/black
*I spent a lot last month and now
I'm in the red.*

_____

in the same boat
*I understand your problem because
you and I are in the same boat.*

_____

in the thick of
*He was in the thick of the fighting,
but was not injured.*

_____

In your dreams.
*'Can I borrow your motorcycle?'
– 'In your dreams.'*

_____

in your shoes
*How would you feel if you were
in my shoes?*

_____

Your language

just like that
I asked her and she said yes – just like that!

_____

keep your head above water
The job is difficult, but I'm keeping my head above water.

_____

keep a straight face
I wanted to laugh, but I managed to keep a straight face.

_____

kick yourself
He kicked himself for forgetting her birthday.

_____

kiss-and-tell
It is a kiss-and-tell book about her affair with the President.

_____

larger than life
The characters in books and films are often larger than life.

_____

leaves me cold
Everyone says it's a great film, but it left me cold.

_____

Your language

let the cat out of the bag
The newspaper let the cat out of the bag before the president's speech.
_____

life in the fast lane
Life in the fast lane is exciting but tiring.
_____

lost for words
The news was so unexpected that he was lost for words.
_____

lost it
Finally, he lost it and threw the computer out of the window.
_____

love at first sight
Their eyes met and it was love at first sight.
_____

make a killing
Umbrella shops make a killing in wet weather.
_____

make ends meet
I can't make ends meet on my very low income.
_____

Your language

make head nor tail of
I can't make head nor tail of this
computer handbook.
_____

make up your mind
You've looked at 12 pairs of shoes.
It's time to make up your mind!
_____

mind's eye
In my mind's eye I'm on a beach
in Barbados.
_____

mind your own business
'How much do you earn?'
– 'Mind your own business.'
_____

miss the boat
She wanted to have children and
was afraid of missing the boat.
_____

Mr Right
'Will I ever find my Mr Right?' she
wondered.
_____

no rocket scientist
He can't understand the instructions
– he's no rocket scientist. عبي/ قليل الاستيعاب _____

Your language

no way
'Do you think they could win?
– 'No way.'

_____

off the cuff
I can't answer that question off
the cuff.

_____

off the hook
He got off the hook because the
police lost the evidence.

_____

on a roll
The company is on a roll. All their
new products have done well.

_____

on a shoestring
He started the business on a
shoestring, working at home.

_____

on board
He's starting a new company and
he wants me on board.

_____

on cloud nine
When she agreed to marry him,
he was on cloud nine.

_____

Your language

on Earth
Where on Earth were you?
What on Earth are you doing?

_____

on edge
I'm always a bit on edge before an
important meeting.

_____

only have eyes for
I'm not interested in him – I only
have eyes for you.

_____

on me
Put your money away. The drinks
are on me.

_____

on the cards
We can't be sure that it'll happen,
but it's on the cards.

_____

on the go
You're always on the go. You should
relax sometimes.

_____

on the line
Fire officers sometimes put their
lives on the line to save others.

_____

Your language

on top of
*We've had problems but we're getting
on top of them now.*

_____

on top of the world
*Yesterday I was on top of the world,
but today I feel miserable.*

_____

over the moon
*That's wonderful news! You must be
over the moon about it.*

_____

pain in the neck
*My little brother can be a pain in
the neck.*

_____

party pooper
*I'm sorry to be a party pooper, but
I don't want to play this game.*

المذعج في الحفلات

pick up the pieces
*After a very bad year, we're picking
up the pieces.*

_____

pick up the tab
*The taxpayer has to pick up the tab
for the government's mistakes.*

_____

Your language

piece of cake
The test was a piece of cake. I got 100%.

_____

play hard to get
Don't you like him or are you playing hard to get?

_____

play it by ear
We don't know what will happen, so we'll have to play it by ear.

_____

pop the question
He pulled out a ring and popped the question.

_____

pull someone's leg
It's not really true. I'm just pulling your leg.

_____

pull strings
He has important friends and can pull strings to get what he wants.

_____

pull the other one
Pull the other one. I know that's not true.

_____

Your language

push the boat out
*People usually push the boat out
when they get married.*
_____

put your feet up
*When I've finished this work, I can
put my feet up.*
_____

put your foot in it
*I'm sorry. I've put my foot in it. I didn't
want to upset you.*
_____

rat race
*She dropped out of the rat race to
become an artist.*
_____

safe bet
*It's a safe bet that we won't win
the Cup.*
_____

score an own goal
*The company scored an own goal
by angering environmentalists.*
_____

see eye to eye
*We don't see eye to eye on politics so
we try to avoid the subject.*
_____

Your language

split their sides
The film was so funny the audience were splitting their sides.

_____

step on it
Step on it!
We're late!

_____

sweep someone off their feet
He swept her off her feet. And now they're married.

_____

take a rain check
Thanks. I can't come tonight, but can I take a rain check?

_____

take some doing
It'll take some doing to carry that piano upstairs.

_____

take to heart
He took the doctor's advice to heart and stopped smoking.

_____

take your time
Take your time. There's no hurry.

_____

Your language

That would be telling.
*We could give you the answer, but
that would be telling.*

_____

that'll be the day
'Is your brother married?'
'That'll be the day!'

_____

the gloves are off
*The gloves are off in the price war
between the two supermarkets.*

_____

the man in the street
*The man in the street wants a
change of government.*

_____

think on your feet
*A soldier has to think on his
feet.*

_____

thumbs down
*The government has given the
thumbs down to a tax cut.*

_____

tie the knot
*After living together for three years,
they decided to tie the knot.*

_____

Your language

to death
What a terrible film. I was bored to death.

_____

to say the least
Skydiving is not the safest sport, to say the least.

_____

touch and go
We won in the end, but it was touch and go until the last minute.

_____

touch base
Touch base with the police and find out if they've discovered anything.

_____

turn a blind eye
Although it's illegal, the police often turn a blind eye to it.

_____

turn heads
It's a fast, stylish car that turns heads.

_____

turn the tables
He managed to get the gun and turn the tables on the robber.

_____

Answers

Review 1

A 1 larger than life = b) exciting
   2 dark horse = a) obscure person
   3 on the go = c) active, busy

B 1 She was so surprised that she was lost for words.
   2 He's too full of himself to be interested in us.
   3 My little brother is a pain in the neck sometimes.
   4 The man in the street cares more about money than politics.

C open answers

Review 2

A 1 on edge = c) anxious
   2 in stitches = a) laughing a lot
   3 lose it = d) be out of control
   4 see red = b) feel very angry

B 1 I feel on top of the world when the sun shines.
   2 She burst out laughing when she saw me.
   3 I'm on cloud nine whenever we're together.
   4 He suddenly hit me. I don't know what got into him.

C open answers

Review 3

A 1 see eye to eye = d) agree
   2 it's on me = c) I'll pay
   3 hit it off = a) like each other
   4 fingers crossed = b) let's hope

B 1 The nice new secretary was a breath of fresh air.
   2 No. You paid last time. This is on me.
   3 I think he has a soft spot for you.
   4 I can't come out tonight, but can I take a rain check?
   5 Give and take is important in a good relationship.

C open answers

Review 4

A 1 no way = b) definitely not
   2 go steady = c) in a regular relationship
   3 he's history = d) in the past
   4 go Dutch = a) share costs

B 1 As soon as they met it was love at first sight.
   2 He took out a ring and popped the question.
   3 Some people plan, others play it by ear.
   4 He's in love and only has eyes for her.

C open answers

D 1 In your dreams!
   2 … a thing about ponytails.

Review 5

A 1 Mr Right = c) the ideal man
   2 hot water = b) trouble
   3 put your feet up = a) relax
   4 off the hook = d) out of trouble

B 1 We're in the same boat, so let's help each other.
   2 You need to get your act together and find a job.
   3 He left the rat race to work in the third world.
   4 How would you feel if you were in my shoes?

C 2, feeling like a fish out of water

Review 6

A 1 two-time = b) be unfaithful
   2 spill the beans = a) reveal a secret
   3 You're telling me. = d) I know that
   4 pulling my leg = c) teasing me

B 1 Look! A spider behind you! – Pull the other one.
   2 What's the secret? – That would be telling.
   3 This is difficult. – You can say that again.
   4 It tastes like Bordeaux. – You've hit the nail on the head.

C open answers

Review 7

A 1 touch and go = a) unsure
2 on the cards = d) likely
3 tie the knot = b) get married
4 have a go = c) try

B 1 We'll have to start again from scratch.
2 Some people can memorise phrases just like that.
3 A golden rule of learning is to practise regularly.
4 It's a safe bet that I'll forget some of these idioms.
5 I couldn't swim at the beginning of the course but now I'm getting the hang of it.

C 1 That'll be the day!
2 … it cut no ice with him at all.

Review 8

A 1 piece of cake = b) easy
2 take your time = c) don't hurry
3 step on it = a) go faster
4 miss the boat = d) be too late

B 1 The police caught the thief red handed.
2 The campaign has started, and the gloves are off.
3 We made a mistake and scored an own goal.
4 The doctor said, 'These pills will do the trick.'

C open answers

Review 9

A 1 off the cuff = b) without preparation
   2 in the red = c) owing money
   3 big fish = d) important person
   4 mind's eye = a) imagination

B 1 I must choose, but I just can't make up my mind.
   2 He started the business at home on a shoestring.
   3 It takes a few days to find your feet in a new job.
   4 My salary is very low, and I can't make ends meet.

C 1 good 2 bad 3 bad 4 good

D 1 … sink or swim.
   2 … got off the ground

Review 10

A 1 below the belt = b) unfair, cruel
   2 up in arms = c) protesting
   3 turn a blind eye = a) ignore it
   4 fall flat = d) fail

B 1 Powerful people can get things by pulling strings.
   2 The plan got the thumbs up/down from the director.
   3 The country has a king, but he doesn't call the shots.
   4 A friendly greeting helps to break the ice.

C open answers

D 1 They laughed so much they almost split their sides.
   2 By 6 pm, the party was getting out of hand.

Other titles available in Penguin Quick Guides

Computer English
English Phrasal Verbs
Descriptions in English
Business English Verbs
Business English Words
Business English Phrases
Making Friends in English
Common Errors in English
Really Useful English Verbs
Really Useful English Words
Really Useful English Grammar